I-cord daisy

**Easy to make but amazingly effective,
these daisies look great round the hem of
a sweater or dress for a vintage 1960s vibe.**

Materials

Oddments of DK yarn
Pair of 3.75mm (UK9:US5)
    double-pointed knitting needles
Darning needle
Contrasting button
Pins

Before you begin

Decide what size flower you want to make and
how many petals you would like. Refer to the chart
below to work out how much I-cord you will need.
Lay the I-cord out flat to measure it, taking care
not to stretch it.

Flower

Cast on 3 sts and work in I-cord (see Techniques,
page 46) until it is long enough for your flower.
Cast off, leaving a long end.

Making up

Use the long yarn end to graft or sew the two
ends of the I-cord together. Fold the I-cord in half
with the joined ends in the centre. Pin the flower
loops to the centre one at a time, making sure
they lie flat and are not twisted. When you are
happy with the effect, sew in place. Attach a
button to the centre.

Length of I-cord

No. of petals	Small flower	Medium flower	Large flower
6	14in (36cm)	19in (48cm)	23½in (60cm)
8	19in (48cm)	25in (64cm)	31½in (80cm)
10	23½in (60cm)	31½in (80cm)	39½in (100cm)
12	28½in (72cm)	37¾in (96cm)	47¼in (120cm)

Tip

If you don't think you can make I-cord, use an old-fashioned knitting dolly for the same effect.

Tip

Knit into the back
of the last stitch on
the first row for
a tidy finish.

Five-petal flower

This versatile flower is so easy to make. Why not brighten up a plain sweater by making a whole bouquet of them in complementary shades?

Materials

DK yarn in main shade
DK yarn in contrasting shade
Pair of 3.75mm (UK9:US5)
    knitting needles
Darning needle
Spare needle or stitch holder

Special abbreviations

Kfb: knit into the front, then the back of the stitch to increase
Skpo: slip one stitch, knit one stitch, pass the slipped stitch over to decrease

Petals (make five)

Using main shade, cast on 4 sts.
Row 1: Kfb, k2, kfb (6 sts).
Row 2: Purl.
Row 3: Kfb, k1, (kfb x 2), k1, kfb (10 sts).
Row 4: Purl.
Row 5: K4, skpo, k4 (9 sts).
Row 6: Purl.
Row 7: (Ssk, k1) three times (6 sts).
Row 8: P2tog three times (3 sts).
Cut yarn and place sts on a spare needle or stitch holder. Make four more petals in the same way, but do not break off the yarn on the final petal.

Centre

Using contrasting yarn, purl across all sts on last petal, then purl across the 12 stitches on the spare needle or stitch holder (15 sts).
Next row: (K2tog, k1) to end (10 sts).
Next row: Purl.
Cut yarn and thread through darning needle, then run through all the sts and draw up tightly.

Making up

Carefully join the centre of the flower, matching the garter stitch ridge. Sew in yarn ends, then press lightly.

Rosebud trim

This ten-minute rose has so many uses. Attach to a hairslide, sew on plain ballet pumps or scatter over the front of a bag – the choice is yours.

Materials

DK yarn
Pair of 3.75mm (UK9:US5)
    knitting needles
Darning needle

Flower

Cast on 55 sts.
Row 1: Knit.
Row 2: (K1, cast off 5 sts) to end.
You should now have 10 sts on the needle.
Break off yarn and thread through all stitches.
Roll the flower round and secure by stitching.
That's it!

Tip

Make an even smaller flower using 4-ply yarn and 2.5mm needles.

Tip

For a long stem, work a longer I-cord and insert a chenille stick down its length.

Carnation

Make your own buttonhole with this design, which is far easier than it looks. You could even make enough to adorn a whole wedding party.

Materials

DK yarn for flower
Green DK or Aran-weight
    yarn for stem
Pair of 3.75mm (UK9:US5)
    knitting needles
Pair of 3.75mm double-pointed
    knitting needles
Chenille stick
Darning needle

Flower

Using 3.75mm needles and yarn, cast on 150 sts.
Row 1: (K1, k2tog) across (100 sts).
Row 2: (K1, k2tog); rep to last st, k1 (67 sts).
Row 3: As row 2 (45 sts).
Row 4: As row 1 (30 sts).
Row 5: As row 1 (20 sts).
Row 6: (K1, k2tog); rep to last 2 sts, k2 (14 sts).
Row 7: As row 6 (10 sts).
Row 8: (K2tog) across (5 sts).
Work 2 rows in garter stitch.
Cast off, leaving a long end.

Stem

Using double-pointed needles and green yarn, cast on 3 sts.
Work in I-cord (see Techniques, page 46) for 3in (7.5cm).
Begin to work back and forth.
Next row: Knit into the front and back of every stitch (6 sts).
Work 5 rows in stocking stitch.
Cast off.

Leaf

Using 3.75mm needles and green yarn, cast on 7 sts.
Cast off 7 sts.
Fasten off, leaving a long end to join it to the stem.

Making up

Cut a 3½in (9cm) length of chenille stick and turn over the ends into tiny loops. Roll the flower into shape, inserting the chenille stick into the stalk formed. Secure by stitching. Wrap the cast-off edge of the stem round the stalk of the flower and join by stitching. Add the leaf halfway down the stem. Sew in the end left when casting on, wrapping it round the tip of the leaf to form a point.

Freeform flower

Simple to make but really striking, this flower is perfect for pinning to the lapel of a plain coat, or as a jaunty addition to the brim of a hat.

Materials

DK yarn in two
    complementary shades
Pair of 3.75mm (UK9:US5)
    knitting needles
Darning needle

Outer flower

Cast on 102 sts.
Rows 1, 3, 5, 7, 9, 11: Knit across.
Row 2: (K1, k2tog) across (68 sts).
Row 4: (K1, k2tog) to last 2 sts, k2 (46 sts).
Row 6: (K1, k2tog) to last st, k1 (31 sts).
Row 8: As row 6 (21 sts).
Row 10: As row 2 (14 sts).
Row 12: As row 4 (10 sts)
Break yarn, leaving a long end.
Thread through rem sts, draw up
and fasten off.

Inner flower

Using different coloured yarn, cast on 102 sts.
Row 1: (K1, k2tog) across (68 sts).
Row 2: (K1, k2tog) to last 2 sts, k2 (46 sts).
Row 3: (K1, k2tog) to last st, k1 (31 sts).
Row 4: As row 3 (21 sts).
Row 5: As row 1 (14 sts).
Row 6: As row 2 (10 sts).

Making up

Join the sides of both flowers. Place the small flower on top of the larger flower, matching the centres. With the yarn used for the larger flower, join the flowers together by working a star shape across the centre, taking the yarn through both layers.

Tip

To match the centres, layer the flowers and insert a knitting needle in the central holes.

Snowflake spirals

These delicate, lacy little flowers are worked in a single piece and grow really fast. They are so easy to make that you'll soon have a whole bunch.

Materials

4-ply or DK yarn
Pair of 3.75mm (UK9:US5)
    knitting needles
Darning needle
Pretty button

Making up

Coil the spiral neatly round a knitting needle until you are happy with the effect. Sew both ends in place using the long end of yarn, then sew the yarn though the centre to secure. Attach a button to the centre of the flower.

Flower

Cast on 16–18 stitches fairly loosely.
Row 1: Knit into the front and back of every stitch.
Row 2: Repeat row 1.
You should now have four times as many stitches as you began with.
Fancy cast-off
*Cast off 2 sts, then slip the last cast-off st back to the left needle
Use this st to cast on 4 more sts.
Repeat cast-off from * across the row.
When only one or two stitches remain on the left needle, cast them off, leaving a long end.

Note: *Don't pull the yarn too tightly when you are making the increases, or it will be difficult to increase on the next row.*

Tip

For a two-layer flower that will sit flatter, cast on 10–12 sts.

Star flower

This large, showy flower makes a real statement and is perfect for showcasing a small amount of leftover novelty yarn.

Materials

DK or Aran-weight yarn
  in main shade
Mohair or novelty yarn
  in contrasting shade
Pair of 3.75mm (UK9:US5)
  knitting needles
Darning needle

Special abbreviation

Yf: yarn forward

Outer flower

Using main shade, cast on 5 sts.
Row 1: K2, yf, k3 (6 sts).
Row 2 and alternate rows: Sl1, knit to end.
Row 3: K2, yf, k4 (7 sts).
Row 5: K2, yf, k5 (8 sts).
Row 7: K2, yf, k6 (9 sts).
Continue in this way until the row: K2, yf, k12 has been worked.
Next row: Cast off 10 sts, knit to end (5 sts on needle).
Rep instructions until 5 petals have been worked, casting off all sts on the final row.
Fasten off.

Inner flower

Using contrasting yarn, cast on 5 sts.
Work as for outer flower until the row: K2, yf, k8 has been worked.
Next row: Cast off 6 sts, knit to end (5 sts on needle).
Rep these rows until 5 petals have been worked, casting off all sts on the final row.
Fasten off.

Centre

Using main shade, cast on 4 sts.
Pattern row: Cast off 3 sts, place rem st on left needle and use to cast on 3 more sts (4 sts on needle).
Repeat until 5 'sprigs' have been worked.
Cast off.

Making up

Join the first 5 sts at the edge of the main flower so the holes line up. Join the gap between the first and fifth petal. Run a length of yarn round the edge of the circle formed, draw up and fasten off. Sew in ends. Repeat with inner flower. Layer the outer and inner flower, staggering the petals, and sew together. Run a gathering thread along the straight edge of the sprigs, join into a circle and gather tightly. Attach to the centre of the flower.

Violets

These pretty flowers can be used singly, made into a corsage by adding a couple of leaves and a pin or made into an everlasting pot plant.

Materials

Green chenille yarn
Purple and yellow DK yarn
Pair of 3.75mm (UK9:US5) knitting needles
Darning needle
Small flower pot and piece of sponge
Scissors
Darning needle

Special abbreviation

M1: make one stitch by picking up the loop of yarn between the stitch just worked and the next stitch, and knitting into the back of it.

Flower

Using purple yarn, cast on 5 sts.
Row 1: * K4, turn.
Row 2: P3, turn.
Row 3: K3, turn.
Row 4: P3, turn.
Row 5: K3, knit into back of st on left needle.
Row 6: P2tog, p1, p2tog (3 sts).
Row 7: Sl1, k2tog, psso (1 st).
Slip the stitch back to the left needle and use it to cast on 4 sts (5 sts on needle).*
Rep from * to * three times more, then rep rows 1–7 once.
Fasten off the last st, leaving a long end.

Making up

Using the long yarn end, oversew down the side of the last petal worked to reach the centre. Fasten off. Lay out the strip of petals, making sure they are not twisted. Take the yarn along to the point of the next petal and pull tight. Repeat until you have gathered all the petals to the centre. Fasten off and join the side. Using yellow yarn, work two French knots (see facing page) in the centre.

Large leaves (make 3)

Using green yarn, cast on 3 sts.
Row 1: Knit.
Row 2: K1, p1, k1.
Row 3: K1, m1, k1, m1, k1 (5 sts).
Row 4: K2, p1, k2.
Row 5: K2, m1, k1, m1, k2 (7 sts).
Row 6: K3, p1, k3.
Row 7: K3, m1, k1, m1, k3 (9 sts).
Row 8: K4, p1, k4.
Row 9: K4, m1, k1, m1, k4 (11 sts).
Keeping pattern as set, work 3 rows straight.
Row 13 (dec): Skpo, k to last 2 sts, k2tog (9 sts).
Row 14: K4, p1, k4.
Row 15: Skpo, k to last 2 sts, k2tog (7 sts).
Row 16: K3, p1, k3.
Row 17: Skpo, k to last 2 sts, k2tog (5 sts).
Row 18: K2, p1, k2.
Row 19: Skpo, k1, k2tog (3 sts).
Row 20: K1, p1, k1.
Row 21: Sl1, k2tog, psso.
Fasten off.

Small leaves (make 3)

Using green yarn, cast on 3 sts.
Row 1: Knit.
Row 2: K1, p1, k1.
Row 3: K1, m1, k1, m1, k1 (5 sts).
Row 4: K2, p1, k2.
Row 5: K2, m1, k1, m1, k2 (7 sts).
Row 6: K3, p1, k3.
Row 7: K3, m1, k1, m1, k3 (9 sts).
Keeping pattern as set, work 3 rows straight.
Row 11 (dec): Skpo, k to last 2 sts, k2tog (7 sts).
Row 12: K3, p1, k3.
Row 13: Skpo, k to last 2 sts, k2tog (5 sts).
Row 14: K2, p1, k2.
Row 15: Skpo, k1, k2tog (3 sts).
Row 16: K1, p1, k1.
Row 17: Sl1, k2tog, psso.
Fasten off.

Making up

Sew in yarn ends and use flowers and leaves as desired.

Pot plant

Use a small plant pot and cut the piece of sponge to fit tightly in the top. Join six leaves together at the centre, alternating large and small leaves. Add a sprinkling of violets in the centre, and sew in place. Sew the bunch of violets through the centre of the sponge and arrange in the flower pot.

French knots

1   Bring needle to RS of fabric. Holding thread taut with finger and thumb of left hand, wind thread once or twice around needle tip.

2   Still holding thread, insert needle tip close to the point where you brought the needle out to the RS of work and pull needle to back so that the twist lies neatly on the fabric surface. Repeat as required.

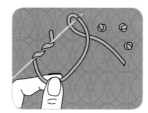 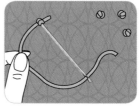

Thistle

Celebrate Scotland's St Andrew's Day on 30 November by pinning this thistle to your lapel – or just wear it because it's so pretty!

Materials

Green DK or Aran-weight yarn
Purple DK yarn
Pair of 3.75mm (UK9:US5)
    double-pointed knitting needles
Darning needle
Sharp scissors
Safety pin

Lower section

Using green yarn, cast on 3 sts and work 2in (5cm) in I-cord (see Techniques, page 46).
Begin to work straight.
Row 1: Knit into the front and the back of every stitch (6 sts).
Row 2: Purl.
Row 3: As row 1 (12 sts).

Flower head

Wind the purple yarn round three fingers 80–100 times.
Tie off the bunch of yarn firmly, then cut the strands to form a tassel.

Making up

Using the ends of yarn used to tie off the tassel, sew it in place at the inside top of the I-cord. Using mattress stitch (see Techniques, page 46), join the sides of the green section. Attach a safety pin along the join by oversewing. Sew in ends. Using very sharp scissors, shape the flower head by cutting straight across.

Hellebores

These delicate blooms can be seen bursting through the snow as one of the first signs of spring. This design captures their fleeting beauty.

Materials

DK yarn in subtle pastel shades
Oddment of green DK yarn for centres
Pair of 3.75mm (UK9:US5) knitting needles
Darning needle
Spare needle or stitch holder
Scissors

Special abbreviations

Kfb: increase by knitting into the front, then the back of the stitch
Ssk: slip one stitch purlwise, slip the next stitch purlwise, knit both stitches together through the back loops

Petals (make 5)

Using pastel yarn, cast on 3 sts.
Row 1: P3.
Row 2: (Kfb) three times (6 sts).
Row 3: Purl.
Row 4: (Kfb) six times (12 sts).
Row 5: Purl.
Row 6: (Ssk, k1) twice, (k2tog, k1) twice (8 sts).
Row 7: Purl.
Row 8: (Ssk twice), (k2tog twice) (4 sts).
Row 9: (P2tog) twice (2 sts).
Break yarn, leaving a long end and place these 2 sts on a spare needle or stitch holder.

Make four more petals in the same way but do not break yarn on the final petal.
Joining the petals
Knit across all petals, thread yarn through and fasten off.

Centre

Using green yarn, cast on 3 sts.
Row 1: Knit.
Row 2: (Kfb) across (6 sts).
Row 3: Knit.
Row 4: Knit.
Row 5: (K2tog) across (3 sts).
Row 6: Sl1, k2tog, psso.

Making up

Using the yarn end, oversew round the edge of the centre to neaten it, then attach to the flower. Sew in yarn ends, using them to neaten the edges of the petals by oversewing if necessary.

Anthers

Thread needle with a length of green yarn. Take yarn through the centre from front to back, make a stitch at the back to secure, then take the yarn up from back to front again. Repeat, spacing the anthers round the edge of the centre. Trim.

Tip

Rub the anthers between your fingers to separate the yarn strands and create a ruffled effect.

Daffodil

Bring a touch of eternal spring to your life with this cheerful flower. It is a little fiddly to make, but it is well worth the effort.

Materials

Yellow, orange and green DK yarn
Pair of 3.25mm (UK10:US3)
    knitting needles
Pair of 3.25mm double-pointed
    knitting needles
Chenille stick
Darning needle
Small pair of pliers
Spare needle or stitch holder

Petals (make 6)

Using 3.25mm needles and yellow yarn,
cast on 7 sts.
Row 1: K1, kfb, k3, kfb, k1 (9 sts).
Row 2: K1, p7, k1.
Row 3: K1, kfb, k to last 2 sts, kfb, k1 (11 sts).
Row 4: K1, p to last st, k1.
Row 5: Ssk, k to last 2 sts, k2tog (9 sts).
Row 6: K1, p to last st, k1.
Row 7: Ssk, k to last 2 sts, k2tog (7 sts).
Row 8: K1, p to last st, k1.
Row 9: Ssk, k to last 2 sts, k2tog (5 sts).
Row 10: K1, p to last st, k1.
Row 11: Ssk, k1, k2tog (3 sts).
Row 12: K1, p1, k1.
Row 13: K1, k2tog, psso.
Fasten off and leave on a stitch holder or spare
needle while you work the remaining petals.

Trumpet

Using 3.25mm needles and orange yarn, cast on
9 sts.
Row 1: Purl.
Row 2: Kfb x 9 (18 sts).
Work 6 rows in k1, p1 rib.
Picot cast-off
(Cast off 2 sts, use st on needle to cast on 1 st);
rep to end of row.
Fasten off.

Stem and stigma

Using double-pointed needles and green yarn,
cast on 4 sts and work 5in (13cm) in I-cord.
Change to yellow for the stigma and work 4 more
rows in I-cord.
Next row of I-cord: K1, k2tog, k1 (3 sts).
Next row: K1, k2tog (2 sts).
Next row: K2tog.
Fasten off.

Leaf

Using 3.25mm needles and green yarn, cast on 3 sts.
Row 1: Knit.
Row 2: K1, p1, k1.
Work until leaf measures 4¾in (12cm).
Next row: K1, sl1, k1, psso (2 sts).
Work 1 row on these 2 sts. Fasten off.

Making up

Flower

Join three of the petals into a triangle by sewing the ends of the cast-on edges together. Run a length of yarn round the edge of the triangle and pull up to make a small circle. Fasten off. Repeat with the remaining three petals. Lay one set of petals on top of the other with the petals staggered. Join the two sets of petals by sewing with tiny stitches.

Stalk

Bend one end of the chenille stick into a tiny loop using the pliers. Ease it carefully through the hole and down the I-cord, lining it up with the petals where the two yarns join. Cut the chenille stick to length, leaving about ½in (1cm) to insert in the stigma. Bend over the end of the stick and ease it up into the stigma. Join the gap and sew in the yarn ends. Insert the stalk through the hole in the centre of the petals and sew in place using tiny stitches.

Trumpet

Join the side of the trumpet. Place over the sepal and join to the centre of the flower, working from the inside to ensure a good finish.

Leaf

Sew in the cast-off end, then attach the leaf to the stem of the daffodil, catching it in place for about 2in (5cm). Bend the stalk of the daffodil so the flower faces forward.

Starch

Make simple starch by dissolving a teaspoon of cornflour (cornstarch) in a jar of water. Wet the petals and allow to dry naturally.

Daisy

This flower is so easy to make, it could be described as a lazy daisy. If you can cast on and cast off, you should be able to make this flower.

Materials

White cotton DK yarn
Oddment of yellow DK or
    Aran yarn for centre
Pair of 2.75mm (UK12:US2)
    knitting needles
Darning needle

Petals (make 2)

Using white yarn, cast on 11 sts.
*Cast off 10 sts (1 st on needle).
Use this stitch to cast on 10 sts.
Rep from * until you have made 12 petals.
Fasten off.
Make another piece the same.

Centre

Lay out one of the strips of petals, making sure it is not twisted. Using yellow yarn, pick up and knit 12 stitches along the edge, working into the 12 holes at the end of the petals.
Row 1: Knit.
Row 2: K1, k2tog across (8 sts).
Row 3: Knit.
Break yarn leaving a long end. Pull up stitches and fasten off. Join the centre into a circle and sew in yarn ends. Do the same with the other strip of petals. Now place the two halves of the daisy wrong sides together, and join by sewing yellow yarn in and out through the holes at the end of the petals.

Poppy

This flamboyant flower has many decorative uses. Mohair gave this version a luxurious look, but it can be worked in wool or cotton yarn.

Materials

Red DK mohair yarn
    (or finer yarn used double)
Green DK yarn
Oddment of black DK yarn
Pair of 3.75mm (UK9:US5)
    knitting needles
Pair of 3.75mm double-pointed
    knitting needles
Darning needle
Safety pin (optional)

Special abbreviations

Kfb: knit into front, then back of stitch to increase
Ssk: slip one stitch purlwise, slip the next stitch purlwise, knit both stitches together through the back loops to decrease
M1: pick up loop between stitch just worked and the next stitch and knit into the back of it to increase

Petals

Using 3.75mm needles and red yarn, cast on 7 sts.
Row 1: Knit.
Row 2: Kfb, k to last st, kfb (9 sts).
Row 3: Kfb, k to last st, kfb (11 sts).
Row 4: Kfb, k to last st, kfb (13 sts).
Rows 5–8: Knit.
Row 9: (Ssk twice), knit to last 4 sts, (k2tog twice) (9 sts).
Rows 10–12: Knit.
Row 13: (Ssk twice), k1, (k2tog twice) (5 sts).
Rows 14–15: Knit.
Row 16: Ssk, k1, k2tog (3 sts).
Row 17: Knit.
Cast off.

Centre

Using 3.75mm needles and black yarn, cast on 15 sts.
Row 1: Knit.
Row 2: (K1, k2tog) across (10 sts).
Join in green and knit 1 row.
Break yarn and thread through all sts. Join centre carefully, matching rows.

Stem

Using double-pointed needles and green yarn, cast on 4 sts and work in I-cord (see Techniques, page 46) for 4in (10cm). Do not cut yarn.

Leaf

Begin to work flat, using the 4 sts of the I-cord.
Row 1: K2, m1, k2 (5 sts).
Row 2: K2, p1, k2.
Row 3: Kfb, k3, kfb (7 sts).
Row 4: K3, p1, k3.
Row 5: Kfb, k5, kfb (9 sts).
Row 6: K4, p1, k4.
Row 7: SSk, k to last 2 sts, k2tog (7 sts).
Row 8: K3, p1, k3.
Row 9: Ssk, k3, k2tog (5 sts).
Row 10: K2, p1, k2.
Row 11: (Kfb twice), k1, (kfb twice) (9 sts).
Row 12: K4, p1, k4.
Row 13: Kfb, k7, kfb (11 sts).
Row 14: K5, p1, k5.
Row 15 (decrease): Ssk, k7, k2tog (9 sts).
Row 16: K4, p1, k4.
Row 17: Ssk, k5, K2tog (7 sts).
Row 18: K3, p1, k3.
Row 19: Ssk, k3, k2tog (5 sts).

Row 20: K2, p1, k2.
Row 21: Ssk, k1, k2tog (3 sts).
Row 22: K1, p1, k1.
Row 23: S1, k2tog, psso.

Making up

Lay the petals out, slightly overlapping, then sew in place. Position the centre and sew in place with small hidden stitches. Stuff the centre slightly using yarn trimmings before closing completely. Sew in yarn ends. Attach the leaf and stem to the back, adding a pin if you want to use the poppy as a brooch (see Thistle, page 20).

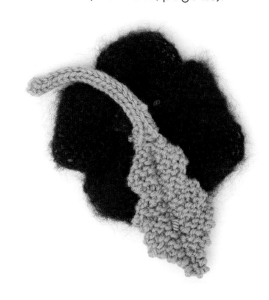

Calla lily

These beautiful, unusual flowers are most often seen in white. Create a real talking point with this stunning pink number.

Materials

Green DK yarn
Pink DK yarn
Oddment of yellow 4-ply yarn
    for stamen
Pair of 3.25mm (UK10:US3)
    double-pointed knitting needles
Pair of 2.75mm (UK12:US2)
    knitting needles
Chenille stick
Darning needle

Stem and flower

Using 3.25mm double-pointed needles and green yarn, cast on 4 sts.
Work in I-cord (see Techniques, page 46) for 8in (20cm) or length desired.
Change to 2.75mm straight needles and knit one row. Take the chenille stick and, using the pliers, bend over one end to make a loop. Push the loop carefully down the length of the I-cord. Neaten the end, sewing through the loop in the wire to keep it in place. Make another loop in the flower end of the wire and push it to the back as you work.
Next row: (P1, purl into the back, then the front of the next st) twice (6 sts).
Break off green, leaving a long end. Join in pink and begin to work flower using 2.75mm needles.

Flower
Row 1: Knit.
Row 2: Purl.
Row 3: Sl1, (kfb) across (11 sts).
Row 4 and every alternate row until row 24: Sl1, purl across.
Row 5: Sl1, (kfb, k1) across (16 sts).
Row 7: Sl1, knit across.
Row 9: Sl1, k3, m1, k4, m1, k4, m1, k4 (19 sts).
Row 11: Sl1, k4, m1, k4, m1, k1, m1, k4, m1, k5 (23 sts).
Row 13: Sl1, k5, m1, k4, m1, k3, m1, k4, m1, k6 (27 sts).
Row 15: sl1, k6, m1, k4, m1, k5, m1, k4, m1, k7 (31 sts).
Row 17: Sl1, k7, m1, k4, m1, k7, m1, k4, m1, k8 (35 sts).
Row 19: Sl1, k8, m1, k4, m1, k4, m1, k1, m1, k4, m1, k4, m1, k9 (41 sts).
Row 21: Sl1, k9, m1, k4, m1, k5, m1, k3, m1, k5, m1, k4, m1, k10 (47 sts).
Row 23: Sl1, knit across.
Row 25: Cast off 6 sts, knit to end (41 sts).
Row 26: Cast off 6 sts, purl to end (35 sts).
Row 27: Cast off 4 sts, knit to end (31 sts).
Row 28: Cast off 4 sts, purl to end (27 sts).
Row 29: Cast off 2 sts, knit to end (25 sts).
Row 30: Cast off 2 sts, purl to end (23 sts)
Row 31: Ssk, k to last 2 sts, k2tog (21 sts).
Row 32: P2tog, p to last 2 sts, p2tog (19 sts).
Now dec one stitch at the beginning of every row until all sts are worked off.
Fasten off.

Stamen

Using 2.75mm needles and yellow yarn, cast on 25 sts and work 7 rows in reverse stocking stitch (see page 46). Cast off, leaving a long yarn end.

Making up

Allow the stamen to roll with the reverse stocking stitch side outermost, and sew along its length using tiny stitches to form a tube. Straighten out the end of the chenille stick and ease the end of the tube over it. Join to the top of the I-cord inside the flower. Using green yarn, close the gap at the top of the I-cord. Allow the edges of the flower to roll inwards; one around the stamen and one across the front of the flower. When you are happy with the effect, catch the front flap in place with a single stitch about 1in (2.5cm) down from the upper rim of the flower. Allow the point of the flower to roll naturally.

Twist the stamen round a spray of real foliage for effect.

Rose corsage

This corsage will cheer up the plainest jacket on a dull day. Chenille gives a stunning effect, but it is just as good worked in mohair or DK yarn.

Materials

Red chenille yarn
Green chenille yarn
Pair of 4mm (UK8:US6)
    knitting needles
Pair of 4mm (UK8:US6)
    double-pointed knitting
    needles
Darning needle
Large safety pin or brooch back

Special abbreviation

M1: make a stitch by picking up the loop of yarn between the stitch just worked and the next stitch and knitting into the back of it

Flower

Using 4mm needles and red yarn, cast on 75 sts very loosely.
Beginning with a purl row and slipping the first stitch of every row, work 10 rows in reverse stocking stitch (one row purl, one row knit).
Row 11: Cast off 5 sts, knit to end (70 sts).
Row 12: Cast off 5 sts, purl to end (65 sts).
Repeat last two rows twice, then row 11 once (40 sts).
Row 18: (K2tog) across row (20 sts).
Cast off.

Leaf (make 2)

Using 4mm needles and green yarn, cast on 3 sts.
Row 1: K1, m1, k1, m1, k1 (5 sts).
Row 2 and every alternate row: Purl.
Row 3: K2, m1, k1, m1, k2 (7 sts).
Row 5: K3, m1, k1, m1, k3 (9 sts).
Row 7: k4, m1, k1, m1, k4 (11 sts).
Row 9 (decrease): Ssk, k7, k2tog (9 sts).
Row 11: Ssk, k5, K2tog (7 sts)
Row 13: Ssk, k3, k2tog (5 sts).
Row 15: Ssk, k1, k2tog (3 sts).
Row 17: K1, p1, k1.
Row 19: S1, k2tog, psso.
Fasten off.

Stem

Using double-pointed needles and green yarn, cast on 3 sts. Work in I-cord (see Techniques, page 46) for length desired.

Making up

Lay the piece of work on a flat surface with the reverse stocking stitch side down, then turn over the top of the flower all round. Roll up loosely with the reverse stocking stitch to the inside. When you are happy with the effect, secure using small hidden stitches all round the rolled lower section. Join the leaves by oversewing all round the edges and attach to the back of the flower. Position and attach the I-cord stem. Sew in yarn ends. Sew on the pin or brooch back.

Tip

If you are using chenille, cast on with a larger size needle as chenille does not stretch.

Bindweed

A weed is simply a plant that is growing in the wrong place. Despite its unattractive name, bindweed is very pretty.

Materials

White cotton-mix yarn
Green DK yarn
Oddment of cream Aran yarn
Pair of 2.75mm (UK12:US2)
    knitting needles
Pair of 3.75mm (UK9:US5)
    double-pointed knitting needles
Scissors
Darning needle

Flower

Using 2.75mm needles and white yarn, cast on 5 sts.
Row 1: Purl.
Row 2: (Kfb) across (10 sts).
Work 3 rows in stocking stitch.
Row 6: (Kfb) across (20 sts).
Work 9 rows in stocking stitch.
Next row: (K1, kfb) across (30 sts).
Work 3 rows in stocking stitch.
Next row: (K2, kfb) across (40 sts).
Work 3 rows in stocking stitch.
Next row: (K3, kfb) across (50 sts).
Work 3 rows in stocking stitch.
Next row: (K4, kfb) across (60 sts).
Change to 3.75mm double-pointed needles and work 3 rows stocking stitch.
Cast off knitwise.

Making up

Join side of flower, allowing the top to roll naturally. Cut four 3in (8cm) lengths of cream Aran yarn and tie a knot near the ends of each. Attach these strands by sewing to the very centre of the flower.

Stalk

Using double-pointed needles and green yarn, cast on 4 sts.
Work in I-cord (see Techniques, page 46) for about 3in (8cm).
Begin to work straight.
Row 1: (Kfb) across (8 sts).
Row 2: Purl.
Row 3: (K1, kfb) across (12 sts).
Row 4: Purl.
Row 5: (K2, kfb) across (16 sts).
Row 6: Purl.
Row 7: (K3, kfb) across (20 sts).
Picot cast off
Cast off 2 sts (use st on needle to cast on 2 sts, cast off 4 sts) to last st.
Cast off final st.
Join side and attach to lower point of flower.

Bluebell

These delicate woodland flowers droop almost as soon as they are picked, but this design will allow you to make a bluebell with lasting appeal.

Materials

Blue and green DK yarn
Oddment of yellow DK yarn
Fine chenille stick
Pair of 2.75mm (UK12:US2) knitting needles
Scissors
Darning needle

Flowers

Large flower (make 4)
Using blue yarn, cast on 12 sts.
Row 1: Knit.
Row 2: Purl.
Row 3: (K2tog, yf) across.
Work 3 rows in stocking stitch.
Row 7: Pick up 1 st from the cast-on hem and 1 st from the left needle and knit the stitches together; repeat across row (see note below).
Work 6 rows in stocking stitch.
Row 14: (P1, p2tog) across (8 sts).
Row 15: Knit.
Break off yarn, thread through rem sts and fasten off, leaving a long yarn end.

Smaller flower (make 2)
Using blue yarn, cast on 12 sts.
Row 1: Knit
Row 2: Purl.
Row 3: (K2tog, yf) across.
Work 3 rows in stocking stitch.

Row 7: Pick up 1 st from the cast-on hem and 1 st from the left needle and knit the stitches together; repeat across row (see note below).
Work 4 rows in stocking stitch.
Row 12: (P1, p2tog) across (8 sts).
Row 13: Knit.
Break off yarn, thread through rem sts and fasten off, leaving a long end.

Note: *If you do not feel you can manage to pick up the stitches, work as a straight knit row and turn back and sew down the picot edge later.*

Bud (make 2–3)
Using blue yarn, cast on 3 sts.
Work 2 rows in stocking stitch.
Row 3: Kfb, k1, kfb (5 sts).
Row 4: Purl.
Row 5: (Kfb, k1) x 2, kfb (8 sts).
Work 4 rows in stocking stitch.
Fasten off, leaving a long end.

Stem

Using double-pointed needles and green yarn, cast on 4 sts and work in I-cord (see Techniques, page 46) for 11in (28cm).
Next row of I-cord: K1, sl1, k1, psso, k1 (3 sts).
Work a further 1½in (4cm) of I-cord on these 3 sts.
Next row: K1, sl1, k1, psso (2 sts).
Next row: K2tog.
Fasten off.

Making up

Stem

Turn over the end of the chenille stick and ease carefully up through the stem from the cast-on end. Draw up and sew in yarn ends. The chenille stick will not reach right to the end of the stem. This is intentional, as the last section of stem is designed to hang.

Flowers

Cut three 3in (8cm) lengths of yellow yarn (2¾in/ 7cm) for smaller flowers) and tie a knot near either end of each length. Lay the lengths parallel and knot together in the centre. Make a similar bundle of stamens for each flower. Take the first flower and sew the knot of a bunch of stamens into the top of the flower, then join down the side using mattress stitch (see page 46). Run the yarn up the inside of the flower and back to the top, ready to attach the flower to the stem. Join the side seam of each bud and run the yarn back to the top as for the flowers. Attach the buds and flowers by sewing each blue yarn end through the stem, leaving about ½in (1cm), then working blanket stitch (see below) along its length. Finish off by knotting lengths of blue yarn at the top of each flower.

Blanket stitch

Working from left to right, bring the needle up at A, down at B and up at C with the yarn looped under the needle. Pull through, taking care to tighten the stitches equally. Repeat from left to right along the length of yarn. Fasten off.

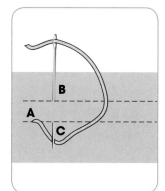
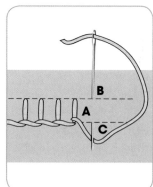

Gerbera

These striking flowers come in many different colours, so it will be easy to use your imagination as well as all those odds and ends of yarn.

Materials

Dark orange DK yarn
Oddments of pale orange
    and black DK yarn
Pair of 2.75mm (UK12:US2)
    knitting needles
Scissors
Darning needle

Petals (make 2)

Using dark orange yarn, cast on 12 sts.
Row 1: K9, yf, sl1, yb, turn.
Row 2: Sl1 p-wise, p to end.
Row 3: Sl1, k5, yf, sl1, yb, turn.
Row 4: Sl1, purl to end.
Cast off 11 sts.
Slip last st from right to left needle and use to cast on 11 more sts.
Repeat rows 1–4 and cast-off/cast-on instructions to make 15 more petals (16 in total).
Cast off.

Centre

Take one of the flower strips and lay it out, making sure it is not twisted and that all the petals are the right way up.
Using pale orange yarn, pick up and knit one stitch from the centre of each of the 16 petals (16 sts).
Row 1: Knit.

Row 2: Knit.
Row 3: (K2tog, k2) across (12 sts).
Row 4: Knit.
Break off pale orange and join in black yarn.
Row 5: Knit.
Row 6: (K2tog, k1) across (8 sts).
Cut yarn, thread the end on a darning needle and pass through the remaining stitches. Pull up tightly, fasten off and join the centre into a circle.

Making up

Turn the flower over and attach the second set of petals behind the first by stitching the centre of each petal to the gap between the first set of petals. Sew in ends. Now damp down the flower and ease the petals gently into shape. Leave to dry naturally.

Tip

For a flatter flower that can be used as an appliqué, omit the second set of petals.

Tip

Clematis can have anything from 5-8 petals - you choose!

Clematis

One of the nicest sights of summer is a clematis scrambling over a wall or trellis. Bring the flowers into your home with this easy-to-make design.

Materials

Purple DK yarn
Oddment of yellow DK yarn
Pair of 3.75mm (UK9:US5) knitting needles
Darning needle
Pencil (optional)

Special abbreviations

Ssk: slip one stitch knitwise, slip the next stitch knitwise, knit both stitches together through the back loops
Kfb: knit into the front then back of the same stitch

Petals

Using purple yarn, cast on 9 sts.
Row 1: K1, ssk, k4, kfb, k1.
Row 2: Sl1, k to end.
Repeat rows 1–2 four times.
Cast off, leaving a long yarn end.
Make a further six petals in the same way.

Centre

Using yelliow yarn, cast on 12 sts.
Row 1: Knit.
Row 2: (K2tog) across (6 sts).
Thread yarn through remaining stitches, pull up and secure.

Making up

Petals
Lay out the petals, making sure they are all the same way up. Take each petal and fold the sides in towards the middle. Join for about ½in (1cm) from one of the points. Repeat with all petals. Lay the petals into a circle with the folded-in sections uppermost and pointing to the centre. Join into a circle by picking up a stitch from the end of each petal and drawing them together. Fasten off.

Centre
Join the side of the centre and neaten if necessary to form a circle. Sew the circle into the middle of the petal cluster, taking care to keep the shape of the pinched sections.

Stamens
Thread a needle with a length of yellow yarn and take it in and out of the centre of the flower to create loops. You may find it helpful to take each strand of yarn round a pencil to create the loops. Take the yarn through to the back and fasten off.

Tulip

This popular flower is available in so many different hues that your only problem will be deciding which one to pick.

Materials

DK yarn in main colour
DK or Aran-weight yarn in green
Oddment of yellow yarn
Pair of 3.75mm double-pointed
    knitted needles
Spare needle or stitch holder
Chenille stick
Small pair of pliers
Darning needle

Stem and first petal

Using green yarn, cast on 5 sts and work in I-cord (see Techniques, page 46) for 8in (20cm).
Begin to work straight.
Next row: (Kfb) x 5 (10 sts).
Next row: Purl.
Next row: Kfb, knit to last st, kfb (12 sts).

Break off green, join in main colour and begin to work petals.
First petal
Row 1: K4, turn leaving 8 rem sts on a spare needle or stitch holder.
Row 2 and alternate rows: K1, p to last st, k1.
Row 3: (Kfb, k1) twice (6 sts).
Row 5: Kfb, k4, kfb (8 sts).
Row 7: Kfb, k6, kfb (10 sts).
Row 9: Kfb, k8, kfb (12 sts).
Row 11: Kfb, k10, kfb (14 sts).
Rows 13 and 15: Knit across.
Row 17: Ssk, k10, k2tog (12 sts).
Row 19: Knit across.
Row 21: Ssk, k8, k2tog (10 sts).
Continue to decrease in this way until there are 4 sts on the needle.
Cast off.
Work the second petal on the next set of 4 sts, and the third petal on the last set of 4 sts.

Inner petals

Cast on 12 sts.
Work one petal as above on each set of 4 sts.

Stamen

Using green yarn, cast on 5 sts and work in I-cord for ¾in (2cm).
Cast off.

Leaf

Using green yarn, cast on 4 sts.
Row 1: Knit.
Row 2: K1, p2, k1.
Repeat the last 2 rows three times.
Next row: K1, m1, k1, m1, k1, m1, k1 (7 sts).
Work 15 rows in stocking stitch, knitting the first and last stitch of each purl row.
Next row: K3, m1, k1, m1, k3 (9 sts).
Work 19 rows on these 9 sts, knitting the first and last st of each purl row.
Next row: K2, ssk, k1, k2tog, k2 (7 sts).
Work 15 rows on these 7 sts.

Next row: K1, ssk, k1, k2tog, k1 (5 sts).
Work 7 rows on these 5 sts.
Next row: K1, ssk, k2tog (3 sts).
Next row: K1, p1, k1.
Next row: Sl1, k2tog, psso.
Fasten off.

Making up

Stem
Using the pliers, bend over the ends of the chenille stick. Working from the cast-on edge of the stem, ease one end gently up through the stem. Ease the short length of I-cord over the other end and sew in place.

Flowers
Press the outer petals individually if desired. Working from the inside of the flower, join each petal to the next for about 1in (2.5cm). Press the strip of inner petals if desired. Join and draw up the edge into a small circle. Ease the circle of petals over the green stamen and sew in place. Finish the flower by adding four short lengths of yellow yarn round the stamen, making a knot in the end of each. Darn in yarn ends.

Tip
For a stiffer leaf, work a length of florists' wire carefully up each side edge.

Damask roses

Make a real statement with these soft, showy blooms in luxurious mohair. Sizes range from small to extra-large, plus buds in two sizes.

Materials

DK-weight mohair yarn:
    1 x 50g ball (approx 109yd/100m)
    makes all six sizes
Pair of 4.5mm (UK7:US7) knitting needles
Pair of 4mm (UK8:US6) knitting needles
Pair of 3.75 (UK9:US5) knitting needles
Spare needle or stitch holder
Darning needle

Tip

When casting on lots of stitches in fluffy yarn, cast on a few spare in case you miscounted.

Flower variations

Flower size	Small bud	Bud	Small	Medium	Large	Extra-large
Sts to cast on	50	66	84	104	126	150
Yarn needed	3g	4g	6g	8g	11g	18g
Measurement	1½in (4cm)	2in (5cm)	2½in (6.5cm)	3in (8cm)	4in (10cm)	4¼in (11cm)

Extra-large rose

Using 4.5mm needles and yarn, cast on 150 sts.
Row 1: K2, k3tog, k4, k3tog, k6, k3tog, k8, k3tog, k10, k3tog, k12, k3tog, k14, k3tog, k16, k3tog, k18, k3tog, k20, k3tog, k10 (130 sts).
Rows 2, 4, 6, 8, 10, 12, 14, 16, 18: P to last 4 sts, turn placing these 4 sts on a spare needle or stitch holder.
Row 3: K2, k3tog, k4, k3tog, k6, k3tog, k8, k3tog, k10, k3tog, k12, k3tog, k14, k3tog, k16, k3tog, k18, k3tog, k9 (108 sts).
Row 5: K2, k3tog, k4, k3tog, k6, k3tog, k8, k3tog, k10, k3tog, k12, k3tog, k14, k3tog, k16, k3tog, k8 (88 sts).
Row 7: K2, k3tog, k4, k3tog, k6, k3tog, k8, k3tog, k10, k3tog, k12, k3tog, k14, k3tog, k7 (70 sts).
Row 9: K2, k3tog, k4, k3tog, k6, k3tog, k8, k3tog, k10, k3tog, k12, k3tog, k6 (54 sts).
Row 11: K2, k3tog, k4, k3tog, k6, k3tog, k8, k3tog, k10, k3tog, k5 (40 sts).
Row 13: K2, k3tog, k4, k3tog, k6, k3tog, k8, k3tog, k4 (28 sts).
Row 15: K2, k3tog, k4, k3tog, k6, k3tog, k3 (18 sts).
Row 17: K2, k3tog, k4, k3tog, k2 (10 sts).
Row 19: K2, k3tog, k1 (4 sts).
Row 20: Purl across all sts, then purl across all the stitches on the holder (40 sts).
Row 21: (K2tog) across (20 sts).
Cast off.

Large rose

Using 4mm needles and yarn, cast on 126 sts.
Follow the instructions on the left from Row 3.

Medium rose

Using 3.75mm needles and yarn, cast on 104 sts.
Follow the instructions on the left from Row 5.

Small rose

Using 3.75mm needles and yarn, cast on 84 sts.
Follow the instructions on the left from Row 7.

Bud

Using 3.75mm needles and yarn, cast on 66 sts.
Follow the instructions on the left from Row 9.

Small bud

Using 3.75mm needles and yarn, cast on 50 sts.
Follow the instructions on the left from Row 11.

Making up

Roll up and secure by stitching, then sew in the yarn ends.

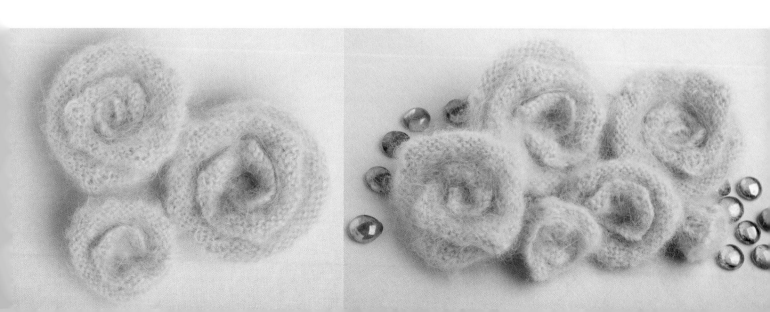

Techniques

Simple cast-on

1 Form a slip knot on the left needle. Insert the right needle into the loop and wrap the yarn around it as shown.

2 Pull the yarn through the first loop to create a new one.

3 Slide the new loop onto the left needle and continue in this way until you have the required number of stitches.

Knit stitch

1 Hold the needle with the cast-on stitches in your left hand. Place the tip of the right needle into the first stitch and wrap the yarn round.

2 Pull the yarn through to create a new loop.

3 Slip the newly made stitch onto the right needle. Continue in the same way for each stitch on the left-hand needle. To start a new row, turn work to swap needles and repeat steps 1–3.

Purl stitch

1 Hold the yarn at the front of the work as shown.

2 Place the right needle into the first stitch from front to back. Wrap the yarn around the needle in an anti-clockwise direction as shown.

3 Bring the needle back through the stitch and pull through.

Stocking stitch

Knit on RS rows and purl on WS rows.
Reverse stocking stitch: purl on RS rows and knit on WS rows.

Garter stitch

Knit every row.

Casting off

1 Knit two stitches, then slip the first stitch over the second and let it drop off the needle.

2 Knit another stitch so there are two stitches on the needle. Repeat steps 1 and 2 until one stitch remains. Break yarn and thread through remaining stitch.

I-cord

Using double-pointed needles, cast on the required number of sts. Do not turn work. Slide sts to the opposite end of the needle, then take the yarn firmly across the back of work. Knit sts again. Repeat to desired length. Cast off, or follow instructions in pattern.

Mattress stitch

Use mattress stitch for an invisible seam and a tidy finish. After pressing, place the pieces side by side with RS facing. Starting at the bottom, secure the yarn and bring the needle up between the first and second stitch on one piece. Find the corresponding point on the other piece and insert the needle there. Keep the sewing-up yarn loose as you work up the seam, then pull tight.

Simple cast-on

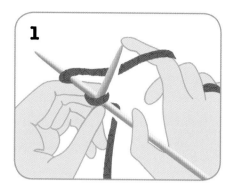

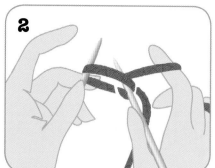

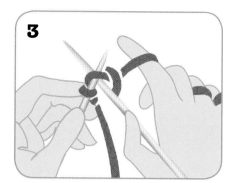

Knit stitch

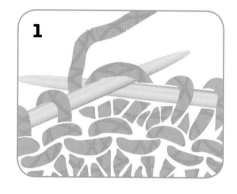

Purl stitch

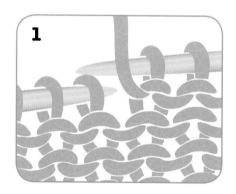

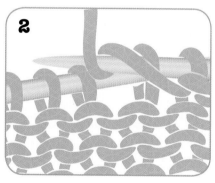

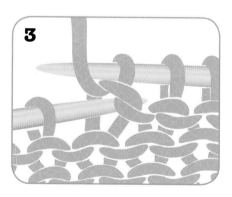

Casting off

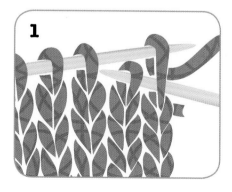

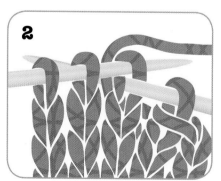

I-cord

Abbreviations

alt	alternate
beg	beginning
cm	centimetres
cont	continue
dec	decrease
DK	double knitting
dpn	double-pointed needle
foll	following
inc	Increase by working into the front, then the back of the stitch
k	knit
k2tog/k3tog	knit two (three) stitches together
p	purl
p2tog	purl two stitches together
psso	pass slipped stitch over
rem	remaining
rep	repeat
sl1	slip one stitch as though to knit it
st(s)	stitch(es)
tog	together
yb	yarn back

Knitting needle sizes

UK	Metric	US
12	2.75mm	2
11	3.25mm	3
10	3.5mm	4
9	3.75mm	5
8	4mm	6
7	4.5mm	7

Note: *It's best to use needles at least a size or two smaller than usual with DK. For ease of working the flowers, it's a good idea to invest in short needles, or work back and forth on double-pointed needles, winding an elastic band round the non-working end to keep the stitches on.*

Simple flower

These easy little flowers can be whipped up in no time using oddments of double knitting yarn. A pearl button centre gives a glamorous touch.

Materials

DK yarn
Pair of 3.75mm (UK9:US5)
    knitting needles
Darning needle
Pearl button

Special abbreviations

Skpo: slip one stitch, knit one stitch, pass slipped stitch over
Kfb: knit into the front, then the back of the stitch to increase

Flower

Cast on 7 sts.
Row 1: Knit.
Row 2: Sl1, k4, k2tog (6 sts).
Row 3: Skpo, k4 (5 sts).
Row 4: Sl1, k2, k2tog (4 sts).
Row 5: Skpo, k2 (3 sts).
Row 6: Sl1, k1, kfb (4 sts).
Row 7: Kfb, k3 (5 sts).
Row 8: Sl1, k3, kfb (6 sts).
Row 9: Kfb, k5 (7 sts).
Row 10: Sl1, k to end.
Rep rows 1–10 twice more, then rows 1–9 again.
Cast off, leaving a long end.

Making up

Join the side of the flower as invisibly as possible and fasten off. Take the long yarn end and thread it through the ends of the rows at the middle of the flower. Pull up the thread and fasten off. Attach a pearl button to the centre.

Tip

Beads from a broken necklace also make excellent flower centres.

Contents

Introduction

These flowers are fast and fun to knit, and amazingly versatile. Best of all, they can be made from really small scraps of yarn. Most of the flowers are made using double knitting (DK) yarn. For best results, use smooth, good-quality yarn. Acrylic tends to be lighter, so it's ideal for flowers on wired stems.